Abandonment. Isolation. Rejection. Abuse. No love.

MAKING MY SPIRIT SMILE

Seeing the Blessing in the Storm

Tiffany Jackson

S.H.E. PUBLISHING, LLC

Copyright © 2021 by Tiffany Jackson.

All rights reserved. Printed in the United States of America. No part of this book may be used or reproduced in any manner whatsoever without written permission except in the case of brief quotations em-bodied in critical articles or reviews.

For information contact: info@shepublishingllc.com
www.shepublishingllc.com

Book and Cover design by S.H.E. PUBLISHING, LLC

ISBNs
Paperback: 978-1-953163-02-8
Hardcover: 978-1-953163-01-1
eBook: 978-1-953163-03-5
SheEdition: 978-1-953163-04-2

First Edition: January 2021

10 9 8 7 6 5 4 3 2 1

Dedication

In honor of my beloved mother, Shirley Graham, who will always make my spirit smile.

Foreword

As I read through MAKING MY SPIRIT SMILE, the word introspection came to mind quite often. Introspection is the examination or observation of one's thoughts and feelings. Tiffany has used the process of reflection to travel back through the good times and the bad of her life to strongly establish herself in the present and secure a healthier emotional future. Knowing her personally and having walked beside her on this journey toward her freedom, I can say that this book has served to open the gates to a life that is filled with passion, purpose, and the light and love of God! A journey like this is not easy and can be filled with twists and turns meant to derail you from the path that God has chosen for you. The narrative that Tiffany walks us through here is evidence of these difficulties. However, the title alone suggests that victory is always possible through Christ Jesus!

My prayer for those who will read this special work is that you, too, will find the courage to travel backward in order to move forward. You have to be willing to always participate in your own rescue, and that is precisely what this author has masterfully done. Proverbs 15:13 says that "A glad heart makes a cheerful face." I believe that through this book, God will remove the callus from your heart for your spirit to truly smile!! Be Blessed!

Bishop Damen M. Bennett
Fresh Oil Ministries, Inc.

Preface

Years ago, I was urged in my spirit to write a book about my life. As the trials and tribulations seemed to overshadow me, this journey of writing my first book seemed to be just a dream. As the years passed, people I encountered spoke and prophesied about my book. However, shame and rejection seemed to play a vital role in the delay of my writing.

The year 2019 would ignite my spirit to be determined, finally and without any distractions, to focus on writing my book. So one evening while sitting on my couch, I heard a soft, clear voice that spoke to me and said, *It is time to write your book, Tiffany.* As I replied to the Lord, I petitioned as to what to title my book. The voice answered, *Making My Spirit Smile.*

I asked, "*Making My Spirit Smile?* What does that mean?"

There were times in your life that were awful and devastating, as the enemy wanted you to focus on all the negativity so you wouldn't fulfill your destiny. However, during those times, there were moments I made your spirit smile, said the Lord. I was so amazed at how I began to recall these "making my spirit smile" moments and how still today the Lord continues to make my spirit smile.

Writing a book was new to me, so I prayed and trusted God to lead me to the right professionals to assist me with my book. One day, while at work, I was having a casual conversation with one of my coworkers, Evita. I told her that I was waiting for the Lord to place a publisher in my midst. She immediately told me about her friend, Shenitha Burton, who is the CEO and founder of S.H.E. Publishing, LLC. Without a doubt, the Lord led me in the right direction—and I'm thankful for Evita and Shenitha for making my spirit smile.

As you read my journey, I will share how God took me from a broken little girl to a bold woman. My heart's desire is for you to find healing, forgiveness, life lessons, purpose, self-worth, peace, and love within the challenging moments within your life. I have been able to tap into my inner self and realize that, while life may have been a roller coaster of events and trauma that suppressed my self-esteem and self-worth, it has also been a journey during which I realized that God has always carried me when I could not walk. Since my conception, He has always made my spirit smile. So as you find your purpose, regardless of trials, tribulations, and disappointments, know that there will be moments amid those storms when the Lord will make your spirit smile. That alone will strengthen you throughout your journey.

Contents

A Child Is Born 1

The Arrival of Abuse and Abandonment 5

My Safe Haven 11

Family Matters 15

Gifts and Gratitude for Silence 21

Deceit, Disbelief & Depression 31

Finding A Piece of Serenity 41

Acceptance and the Special In Me 47

Unconditional Love 53

A Child Is Born

Jeremiah 1:5, New Living Translation

I knew you before I formed you in your mother's womb. Before you were born, I set you apart and appointed you as my prophet to the nations.

The strength to smile despite my past traumas, disappointments, and regrets came from a powerful source of inspiration. While smiling on the outside to give the false appearance of happiness, an image men and women have portrayed throughout history, my soul cried out, *I'm dying.* So I asked myself, *How can a dark-skinned, big-eyed, skinny little insecure country girl experience a smile within her soul?*

The time was 12:35 p.m. on December 9, 1971. It was a cold winter's day in the city of Cleveland, Ohio. A beautiful baby girl was born to Shirley Jean Johnson and Bennie Eddie Jackson. The first moment of making my spirit smile was the birth of me, Tiffany Zabrina Jackson.

As a child, I heard about the Trinity—God, Jesus, and the Holy Spirit—in Sunday school. I knew there was a God, but I didn't know the mysteries and the depths of God. I wasn't a religious child, but I did go to church services every Sunday. However, my connection to God wasn't about going to church. Instead, it was about having an open heart, spirit, and personal relationship with Him. I can't explain it, but I knew I was being guided by a higher being, even though God was invisible to my natural eye.

The spirit of man is not a label or denomination, but my spirit has been drawn by the loving pull of God. My heart allowed me to receive strength, comfort, and correction from God in whom I find my peace and serenity. Unbeknownst to me, God's love was making room in my heart for Him.

As I grew from child to adolescent, then to teenager, I struggled with seeing myself through the lens God saw me. The pain had distorted my view and made it hard for me to find joy. Through the cracks of my brokenness, which I will reveal, I heard the spirit of God say, *Here is where your joy lies*. The pleasure and self-acceptance I looked for rested in His word. I felt different from the time of birth. I never felt like I could relate or adapt to others. I was the chosen one to experience the obstacles of a complicated life that would become a testimony that I'd one day share. Now I know isolation comes with uniqueness.

> **Here's a Making My Spirit Smile Moment:**
>
> When I was a little girl, I thought that babies were born through the navel. I recall asking my mother as I pointed to her belly button, saying, "This is where babies come from."

The Arrival of Abuse and Abandonment

Psalm 13:1–2, Good News Translation

How much longer will you forget me, Lord? Forever?
How much longer will you hide from me?

I often daydream about my childhood. My mother left my brother and me with my grandparents. I guess she figured this would be the best thing for us. She was in and out of my childhood life for reasons unknown at the time. My father was not around either, and because of this, I felt and struggled with abandonment. The domino effect of abandonment followed by physical abuse—which then led to verbal and sexual abuse—would influence my adulthood and create a depression I began to feel growing up. I became a depressed child, but again, something within me kept me striving and gave me a sense that this, too, shall pass.

When my mother would visit, I'd love those moments because she would show me and tell me she loved me. My mother spent quality time with us when we saw her. I remember when my mom would come into the house, she would pick me up and hug me. My grandmother would tell her to put me down as if I were too big for that. No matter what happened, whether she stayed for one day, many days, or left, I'd always have that love for her. My mother was the first woman I loved who made my spirit smile. Not to mention the word of God says that we must honor our parents. So as I grew up, whether my mother or father was there or not, I was always taught to honor my parents.

My grandmother was very overprotective of us. Once, my mom came to the school my brother Bennie and I attended and said she was taking us to our grandmother's house. We were so surprised and happy to see her. At that time, we attended Hickory Elementary School and I must have been in the third or fourth grade. All I know is we ended up on a Greyhound bus and on our way to California. When my brother and I didn't come home from school, I'm assuming my grandparents became worried. So my grandmother sent my grandfather, John, to the school and he found out that my mother had picked us up and taken us with her. My grandmother was furious. However, we ended up back with my grandmother because my mother wanted to attend nursing school and she needed the extra help again.

Living with my grandparents, I never heard the words "I love you" from them. I never had a slumber party, birthday party, celebration when promoted to the next grade, or merely a good deed celebrated. My grandmother didn't even discuss sexual development or sex education with me. I remember I was taking a bath and I saw the water turning light red. I was terrified because I thought I had harmed myself without realizing. I was afraid to say anything, but my grandmother asked, "Are you bleeding?"

I answered, "Yes!" I still wasn't sure what was going on until I heard my school peers mention it. As a matter of fact, one of my cousins asked me about my menstrual cycle, and from there she explained everything to me.

Seeking Understanding of Grandma
Although I didn't really understand some of my grandmother's ways, I think you'd have to know a little about the life of my grandmother to totally understand the

place from where she had come. My grandmother was raised in a household where the woman maintained the home and nurtured the children while the men worked. My grandmother did not have an education because during that time she was a sharecropper, which means she spent most of her childhood picking cotton. The women during that time didn't have a voice. When they were told to do something, they did it. I always heard the phrase, *There are two jobs for a woman: in the kitchen, and in the bedroom.* As a matter of fact, my grandmother didn't choose to marry my grandfather. She was told who to marry, and he was the one selected for her. The marriage was arranged and not derived from a place of love. So to reassure my grandmother of my love for her, I wrote letters throughout my childhood to her. I would write down how I felt about her and I would tell her in those letters that I loved her.

How can someone who never heard the words "I love you" know how to love or know if they are being loved? A person only can give you what was given to them. Remembering back to a few moments shared with my grandmother, I realize that is the only way she knew how to love, but during my childhood growing up, I did not understand that. When most have the expectation of seeking healthy physical and emotional ties from the primary source of their family, the cycle of rejection was becoming more real and ingrained in my heart.

Today, I still believe there is a mystery in discovering how you can truly love someone who doesn't reciprocate that emotion in their actions. Some might say that my grandmother provided for my brother and me and that is love. To my children, I want to ensure they know I love them, and to the world, I want people to feel the flow of love from me through my words and my actions. I almost feel like I should have been a veterinarian. People weren't around, but the animals were everywhere. I would nurse our sick cats back to health, and if I'd see a falling caterpillar, I would place it back upon the tree. Love is powerful without conditions. If love comes with conditions, that, to me, isn't love.

There were moments where I felt isolated and alone in the flesh, and there was a period of time when I felt the Lord's presence wasn't with me. I needed someone to hear me screaming with a bold sign without me verbally expressing my thoughts. However, something that I couldn't explain was how I had the stamina to push through life and continue moving forward, but spiritually I felt secure because I was becoming aware of the Holy Spirit during the lessons presented and discussed at the church I attended.

Here's a Making My Spirit Smile Moment:

Every spring, I can remember right before the rain would drop and the wind would blow, I'd go outside and start dancing to show the love I felt for God. I would imagine myself as a ballet dancer. I even pretended to have an audience at my outside performances. This was my way of expressing my love for the Lord without saying a word. In my mind, at that moment, I felt that God's eyes were upon me. I later learned about the scripture of King David dancing before the Lord, and this was something that my spirit was urged to do—just as he had done. My dancing was my offering to God. I loved this time of the year because while I danced, I always spoke passionately to the Lord. I felt strengthened, free-spirited, and loved. It was like God was smiling upon me. I couldn't understand why I felt connected to the Lord, as the only time the Lord was discussed in my home was on Sunday morning.

My Safe Haven

Psalm 27:5, ESV

For he will hide me in his shelter in the day of trouble; he will conceal me under the cover of his tent; he will lift me high upon a rock.

School became my safe haven. I was able to be free, be me, and take out on others what was happening to me at home. While at school, I didn't focus on my academics. I was a class clown. I'd have uncontrollable outbursts of bad behavior, and I acted out to the point where I became a danger to myself. I had so much rage inside of me that anything would trigger me to get angry. I would physically attack anyone at the drop of a dime. The teachers were even afraid of me.

During the 1970s and early 1980s, the school district passed a law for teachers and staff to inflict physical punishment in the form of paddling, or striking on the buttocks. I was subjected to this form of physical punishment when I displayed bad behavior at school, but being in that schoolhouse still was not as bad as the abuse I encountered at home. So when I got into one of my moods and I began biting, kicking, and pushing tables, I was not only subjected to this form of physical punishment, but I was put into a closet because I had become so infuriated. That certainly didn't help me straighten up, nor did it make me want to do right.

I realize now that children of abuse will act out in a way to reflect how they are hurting, and I was hurting. That malicious behavior I expressed and displayed certainly detoured the core reasons of my problems, and this was not good at all.

Home

As I returned home from acting out at school, I would receive three times a beating with extension cords and switches. I was also called unthinkable names: stupid, dumb, and ugly. By the time I reached the age of nine, I had encountered horrible abuse from my grandmother. This treatment happened to me all the way up to the age of twelve. Because of the way I was treated at home, it provoked me to continue my bad behavior at school. I felt like I was a mistake and a tool for life to beat. I was living in the darkness and I felt empty. It was to the point where I became very hyper, which society would label as an attention deficit disorder.

Church

Church also became my safe haven. I attended Bethel Baptist Church in Hickory, Mississippi. It was a small congregation. I would enter through the double doors, walk to my seat on the wooden pew, and I'd watch the pastor as he stood behind the pulpit. I'd listen as he interpreted the scriptures and discussed the Holy Spirit in depth. I also participated in the choir, which I enjoyed, and I was a youth usher providing service with a smile. In church, I got baptized, although I didn't completely understand what it meant. I did feel God's spirit. I'd cried out to the Lord, and when I felt his presence upon me, my eyes filled with tears.

One Sunday at church, I recall running outside and finding a writing pen with a built-in timer. I gave the pen to my pastor, and he made an announcement during church services to see if anyone would claim it. No one came forth, so the pastor looked at me and said, "You can have the pen, Tiffany." As the pastor proceeded to give me the pen, my grandmother took it. She stated in front of everyone that I was so stupid that I didn't need it. I remember this like it was yesterday. As I stood there in my white floral dress and black slippers, I felt worthless, embarrassed, and ashamed. As my eyes filled with tears, I refused to let the tears flow down my face. Although I suppressed those emotions and I was truly hurt, being in church and around other positive influences kept my spirit smiling.

Here's a Making My Spirit Smile Moment:

Each week at school, our homeroom class would challenge other homeroom classes in sports and academics. My classroom was passionate about this. We would have fun, but we were serious when it came to competition. We were determined to remain number one when it came to academic and sports challenges, and this was a moment when everyone was on the same accord and encouraged their teammates.

Family Matters

1 Timothy 5:8, KJV

But if any provide not for his own, and specially for those of his own house, he hath denied the faith, and is worse than an infidel.

Beloved Aunt Jane, my grandfather's sister, lived up on the hill from our home. Aunt Jane was gentle, positive, kind, and she never had anything negative to say about anyone. Every time I felt alone or bored, I would go to my Aunt Jane's house. I would sit on the porch, and she would come out to join me. I remember her telling me to be a good girl so that I wouldn't get a whupping. She would tell me how pretty I was, but she also told me how disobedient I was. She was always honest with me, so I felt a sense of love from her.

My Brother Bennie

My brother Bennie was the middle child. Keep in mind I was the baby girl and always looked out for my brothers. Bennie was more on the quiet side compared to me. He would still play with me—as long as we weren't playing with my baby dolls. "Girlie games," as he would say. My brother Bennie wasn't worried about me in school because he knew I wouldn't let anyone bully me, or him, for that matter. Bennie was quiet, but don't underestimate him. Today he is such an inspiration to me as he has become a businessman in Salem, Alabama.

One of the best times that I remember was Christmas. My brother Bennie and I would get a large, brown paper bag full of apples, oranges, nuts, and a giant, thick peppermint stick. Even though we didn't receive what most children received, that was a happy moment for me, and it represented a form of love. Another Christmas memory is when my mother sent money to my grandmother to purchase our bikes. My brother and I didn't know how to ride bikes. During the Christmas break, we would go up this hill from our Aunt Jane's house. The hill was very steep, and it would allow us to speed. My brother went down the hill first and was focusing on pedaling and keeping the bike steady. He did very well without falling.

MAKING MY SPIRIT SMILE

Now it was my turn. Keep in mind we did not have any protective gear. I was nervous with excitement. My brother must have sensed my nervousness, because as I was rolling down the hill, my brother was running beside me. He was trying to help me stay upright and keep the bike straight. As we approached downhill, I lost control of the bike and was headed toward a ditch. Yes! I landed in the ditch. Even though I wasn't hurt, at that moment it wasn't funny and I was so afraid. As adults, however, my brother and I reflect on that scene and rejoice in laughter over it.

    I remember this classmate of Bennie's came over to visit after school. We were not allowed to have visitors at all. I was timid when it came to boys. I remember that my brother was outside, and I was inside my room, working on my homework. I was sitting on my bed, and my brother's friend came and sat next to me. He started fondling and touching me in inappropriate places. I didn't know what to do because this had never happened to me.

    My brother's friend continued to do this for a couple of weeks. When I saw him at school, he went about as if nothing had happened between us. The girls would fight over him, not knowing I couldn't stand the sight of him. Today he is a functioning alcoholic. I have forgiven him because his father used to beat him and his sister. I recalled many times him and his sister coming to school with bruises on them—and once a broken arm. At that time, I was mature in that I could connect the dots; I was just afraid to tell.

Joyce

I remember when I was five or six years old, there was a friendly neighbor named Joyce who lived down the road. She was the most loving, kind, and beautiful person I'd ever met. In a sense, she reminded me of my mother. Her entire family was very kind toward my family. Every time I saw Joyce, I'd run down the road to greet her. My grandparents and other family members would instruct me time after time not to run down to Joyce's home because to get to there I had to run down a dirt road. They wanted to ensure our safety. Although this was the case, I still didn't listen. And even though my grandparents and other family members told me they'd punish me for going, they never did. I'd continued to run down that dusty road, bubbling with excitement to hug Joyce. She would be standing there with open arms and tell me to go back before I got into trouble. Joyce is full of love, and as of today, we still rejoice over those times, and she continues to make my spirit smile.

MAKING MY SPIRIT SMILE

The Neighbor

Another time, one of my neighbors called me over to his mobile home and asked me to come in. I entered, and he started to hug me. Before this, he was very kind and never gave me a notion of the behavior he was about to display. He sat down and wanted me to sit on his lap, which I did because I wasn't aware of the signs of an abusive man. While I was sitting on his lap, he was trying to penetrate me (I didn't realize this until I got older). My grandfather began calling me from the house. As I was leaving, he told me to tell my grandfather he wanted to borrow a hammer. My grandfather gave me the hammer to take back to him. As I brought him the hammer, he had the nerve to wink at me. I gave it to him and left, running back to the house.

Here's a Making My Spirit Smile Moment:

I recall being at Aunt Jane's House. Beautiful Aunt Jane was never married and would spend most of her time at home. If I did something wrong, she would say, "I'm going to whup you," but she never did. When I would get severely beaten by my grandmother, Jane would comfort me. She would hug me and tell me not to cry. Every Sunday, Aunt Jane would put on her makeup and be dressed sharply to go nowhere. She never had the desire to be married. Aunt Jane lived till her late nineties. I also remember the song "Let's Hear It for the Boy" by Deniece Williams coming on. I liked that song. So I would do cheerleading routines with backbends and summersaults.

Gifts and Gratitude for Silence

Proverbs 22:7, ESV
The rich rules over the poor, and the borrower is the slave of the lender.

Growing up in a small country town, I would see people abusing their kids by calling them names in public. I would also notice that kids I went to school with would come to school with broken arms or legs and black eyes, which seemed to be accepted. What's astonishing is how it looks like adults in the past and presently don't get to the root cause of the problem when it comes to the children.

You would think that I would be isolated or withdrawn when dealing with the public because of my circumstances, but that was the complete opposite in my case. I still wanted friends and I tried to connect with people. I wanted to show love and be social. I didn't want people to know what was happening to me behind closed doors. Plus, I didn't want anyone to blame me for being the cause of what was happening to me.

Twenty Dollar Bill

I was very close to my grandfather. He'd give me my way most of the time. He might have threatened to punish me, but he hardly did. I remember an older Caucasian male associate of my grandfather who would come to visit on the weekends. I remember him coming over, and my grandfather and I were sitting at the kitchen table. He sat in a seat near me, and while he was talking to my grandfather, he put his hand underneath the table and began touching my vagina. I was a deer caught in headlights. I couldn't believe it. This man had excellent standing in our community, and this is what he was doing to me? Finally, he left, and I felt a void; empty, and shameful. I was violated.

During the era in which I grew up, when someone from another race visited a lower-class, poor black family, that would mean you're thought of a great deal. My grandfather was a very loving and respectable man in the community. During the second visit of my grandfather's Caucasian friend, which was the following weekend, he entered our home and greeted my grandfather and me with a hello, in addition to hugging me. I didn't want to hug him. He was telling my grandfather and me how big I was getting. Instead of him letting me go, he sat down with me in his lap. This man was molesting me. How he was able to touch me discreetly, I don't know. As he left he sneakily handed me a twenty dollar bill, and I never saw this man again.

I couldn't believe it. Twenty dollars was like one hundred dollars to me at that time. No one had ever given me that much money before. That was the most money I had ever seen. That week, I stopped by the store on my way to school to buy some candy for my brother and me. I bought enough to share with my friends too. I didn't tell my brother, nor did he ask where the money came from. I knew if my grandmother found out, I would get a beating because she would have thought I stole the money.

As a child, I didn't fully understand the purpose of him giving me the money, and I couldn't understand how he thought he could do this to me. As an adult, I realize this is what pedophiles do to keep their victims silent. They will use fame, money, and material things to silence their victims. Cash and gifts are eye candy for those who are feebleminded. Sexual abusers seek out those who they can manipulate, those labeled as high-risk problem children in a broken home without a solid family foundation. They will seek out their prey, violate them, and reward them for allowing them to do what they think they have the right to do. The money will give you mixed emotions. By accepting the money, I felt that what the abuser did was acceptable. And it is not—please speak up and tell someone. If you find yourself in a particular environment as I did—reach out to a family member, a teacher, neighbor, or church community. If not, this cycle of abuse will follow you and attract other predators to harm you. I know this firsthand.

Heading to California

As I reached the end of the sixth grade, my grandmother had a heart attack. She was unable to care for me. Therefore, my mother arranged for me to come to California with her. My brother Bennie remained in Hickory, Mississippi, to assist with my grandparents' daily living. I was twelve years old, and leaving was a bittersweet moment. Even though I experienced trauma and disappointments in Hickory, I felt a sense of attachment and loyalty. Back home in Hickory, we only had access to two television channels. In California, we had cable access.

MAKING MY SPIRIT SMILE

One day as I was scrolling through the channels, I saw a title: *Little House on the Prairie*. I watched one episode, and I have been hooked ever since, maybe because the setting reminded me of being home in Hickory, Mississippi.

So when I arrived in Sylmar, California during the summer of 1984, this was a cultural shock. Everything was at such a fast-moving pace. My mother was living with this man named Willie Lawson. Unlike my previous experiences with men, this seemed to be different. Mr. Lawson was a loving, educated, and articulate man. He treated me like his own daughter. Mr. Lawson introduced me to black history and a wide variety of black culture, and he stressed the importance of knowing your history.

1 Corinthians 13:13, God's Word Translation
"So these three things remain: faith, hope, and love. But the best one of these is love."

Could it be that someone could love me? Could it be that a man can love me like a daughter without hurting me? When you think love is only in your imagination, the Lord will always show up on the scene. I was still dealing with abandonment issues with my mother. At times I would be happy, and then a sense of depression would come over me.

The Only Real Father I Knew

I was very withdrawn and depressed, and Mr. Lawson always uplifted me with his kind words. He sensed that I was an unhappy little girl. I struggled with feeling unworthy of love. I never had a positive male role model in my life. Mr. Lawson was a man of integrity. However, I still couldn't comprehend how anyone genuinely could love me. He knew that I was a broken little girl and he tried to restore love and hope within me.

That summer, I met a girl who would become a friend of mine. Her name was Chrissy, and she didn't live in the neighborhood. She was only there because she was visiting her grandmother as she usually did every other weekend. Chrissy was about two years younger than me, but she was very feisty and she loved people. Mr. Lawson always talked about Chrissy because she would stop and talk to him while skating down the sidewalk. I didn't know how to skate. Chrissy would take her skates off and let me put them on. She would hold my hands while I tried to stand and roll in them, and this reminded me of the time my brother and I were trying to learn how to ride a bike. I was determined to conquer skating, which I did.

MAKING MY SPIRIT SMILE

The Goodwill

The fall of 1984 was the beginning of my seventh-grade year of school. Olive Vista Middle School was about two miles away from where we lived. I was very nervous about attending this school. I didn't meet anyone who truly wanted to be my friend, and I have always felt different. Because of my southern accent, every time I spoke, I was mocked by my classmates. I never fit into the "in" crowd. My mother bought my clothing from the nearest Goodwill, and I thought the Goodwill was where everyone shopped until I spoke about where my mother got my clothing. That wasn't a great idea because I began getting teased about my dress. I was constantly bullied, but instead of acting out physically, I would act out by talking when the teacher was speaking, acting like a class clown, disrupting the classroom, skipping class, and not completing my assignments. I couldn't control my insecurities and emotions, not realizing there was a good chance that I was holding some anger deep inside myself and suppressing emotions or behavior that was never addressed.

One day after school, I didn't come home. I can't explain why, but I didn't. I remained out until the next day when I went home. My mother reported me missing. When I arrived home, Mr. Lawson was there and he was relieved to see me. He asked me why I did that. I did not answer; I just completely shut down. I was numb and had no feeling of remorse or regrets about anything. It was like there was an evil force within me and I could not control it.

As the days passed by, everything was moving along like usual. At some point during my mother and Mr. Lawson's time together, their relationship seemed to be at a standstill. As I recall, one evening my mother, Mr. Lawson, and I were in the den. Mr. Lawson was discussing with my mother why they were going their separate ways and he was a bit sad about the situation. He told my mother he'd found out she cheated on him while he was out of town, but he wasn't really away. He'd hired a private investigator to spy on my mother, and they reported that my mother was having an affair. My mother seemed shocked, and I was sitting in silence.

My mother and I had to move out of his home. Now keep in mind Mr. Lawson was a positive and loving father figure for me. My mother found an apartment for us; two bedrooms and two baths. The Courtyard apartments were located about fifteen minutes from where Mr. Lawson stayed, and this was a new adjustment for all of us. My mother seemed to be sad about the breakup with Mr. Lawson. As usual, I was going through the motions.

MAKING MY SPIRIT SMILE

Here's a Making My Spirit Smile Moment:

Some people think being an only child or the only child in the household is all good. At times you will become lonely. So Mr. Lawson would take me to Northridge Skateland roller-skating rink, which was a happy place for me. Everyone was on the same accord. The enjoyment of skating made me feel as if this was a place where I belonged.

Deceit, Disbelief & Depression

1 Peter 5:8, NIV

Be alert and of sober mind. Your enemy the devil prowls around like a roaring lion looking for someone to devour.

The devil was after me, and I allowed him in. My mother became so fed up with my behavior, to the point where she bought me a one-way ticket to Cleveland, Ohio. I was placed onto a plane to be with a man I hadn't seen in years: my father. When I arrived at the airport, I didn't know what to do or where to go. I roamed all day 'til night. Finally, two airport officers took notice. They took me to a room and began to question me. I told them about the situation, I gave them my dad's name, and they were able to contact him. He then came to the airport and picked me up.

As we were driving from the airport, his main concern was about my mother and not me. He kept asking me questions about her. Now keep in mind my mother didn't keep my father from us. It was his choice not to stay connected with us. Upon arrival at his home, he introduced me to his wife and their two children. It seemed as if they were excited to see me. I wasn't happy at all. I was just going through the motions.

Ohio was very depressing. I was unable to adapt to my surroundings. That evening I recall wanting to watch wrestling, but I could not watch it because there was only one television in the household. At that time I was a huge Hulk Hogan fan. Therefore, I said good night and I proceeded to the bedroom. As I was preparing to undress, my father entered the room. He was asking me several casual questions. One of the questions he asked me was if I had a boyfriend.

I replied, "No."

He then asked me if I'd ever seen a penis before. He used the other word.

I replied again, "No."

At that moment, a feeling of discomfort came over me. He asked for a hug, and his hug was very inappropriate for a father and daughter. He said, "You need to know how

MAKING MY SPIRIT SMILE

a d**k feels." He placed my hand onto his penis and began rubbing it back and forth. He touched my breast, and all I wanted to do was drop dead. He continued until he got his thrill, and as he left the room, I felt numb and forgotten.

    I thought things would be better in Ohio. It seemed like one crisis after another. The following morning, he acted as if nothing happened, and the next evening, I ran away. I tore the screen off the door and left. I didn't know where I was heading, but my mind was set on going far away from there. About thirty minutes later, my father found me. He ordered me to the car, and I refused. It was nighttime, and people in the area were watching as we went back and forth. He started to drag me into the car, and I got loose. Someone called the police, and when the police arrived, I told them what happened the prior evening. For some reason, the police didn't take any action against my father. The officer then ordered me to go home with him.

    The next morning, my father drove me to the airport, sending me back to my mother. I boarded the plane, and before takeoff my father came onto the flight to say goodbye. That was the last time I spoke to and saw my father. Later in life, I wondered if he had done what he'd done to me to his other children, and as of today, I wonder if he is living or deceased.

Foster Care

I arrived back at LAX and wandered throughout the airport the entire day. My mom didn't have a clue I was coming back. That evening the security from the airport approached me and asked me if I was waiting for someone. It was a replay of when I had landed in Ohio, but I was now back in California. I informed them of the situation that had happened, I gave them my mother's information, and they called her. My mother refused to come to pick me up, so the Department of Children and Family Services was contacted on my behalf.

That evening I was placed into a foster care home located in South Central Los Angeles. We drove up to a reddish brick house with white trim and a nice-sized yard, and we were greeted by Mr. and Mrs. Henderson. They seemed like pleasant folks. Mrs. Henderson seemed like a very nice, kind, and loving woman, and Junior, Mrs. Henderson's husband, looked to be about ten years younger than she was. There were other girls in the home. They were very nice to me, and Mrs. Henderson had two sons that lived in the guest house. As I began to get settled, Mrs. Henderson did all that she could to make me comfortable. She informed me of the chores each girl was responsible for, and during the end of the week, Mrs. Henderson gave each of us an allowance. On some weekends, some of the girls were allowed to visit relatives. Therefore, this left me alone in the house with Mr. and Mrs. Henderson.

One weekend I was home watching television in the family room. The other girls were away. As I sat on the couch, watching TV, Junior came over and we began to chat. All of a sudden, he began pacing around the room. At first, I didn't pay much attention to it because Junior was always walking as if he were in a hurry. The next thing I knew, he took my hand and led me to the room near the front entrance. I was saying to myself, *What is he doing?* He didn't say anything at that moment. He placed me onto the corner table, which was against the wall, pushed me down, and started removing my undergarments. As he was doing this, I was staring at the door, hoping someone would come in and catch him. I feared no one would believe what this man was doing to me. He started to perform oral sex on me. Here I was again, numb and having an out-of-body experience. I wanted to die. I was not mentally present, and I began tearing up with no understanding of why this was happening to me again.

I could hear Mrs. Henderson coming into the house from the kitchen, which was located in the back of the house. Junior hurriedly got off of me and ran down the hall to his bedroom. I stood up and went into the living room as if nothing had happened. Mrs. Henderson began to speak. She asked me how I was doing. I told her I was okay, even though my face might have said something different. I realized she didn't even sense that something was not right because I was unhappy most of the time, and in her eyes, this day was no different.

People must pay attention to their loved ones and recognize the signs when something isn't right with them. Even though verbally someone might say they're okay, read between the lines. Look at their body language; are they acting withdrawn, depressed, or angry; do they feel isolated; and so on. But again, at that moment, talking with Mrs. Henderson, my outer appearance was the norm for her, but my inner being was in torment.

The other girls were very disrespectful to Junior, not to mention it was irritating to see him walking around the house shirtless with his alcoholic beverages. Since the other girls would talk back to him, I saw a loophole that I dived into. Every time Junior would say something to me or the other girls, I would embarrass him or say something disrespectful. The other girls would laugh and they thought it was funny. The other girls would never connect the dots as to why I was so mean to him. Mrs. Henderson remained clueless about the reason I was so mean to her husband.

She did address me and the other girls about being disrespectful, but I didn't care because she had no idea how he violated me.

One day during the week, I was in my room, and my room was located in the back of the house next to Mrs. Henderson and Junior's room. There was a connecting door from their room to mine. Junior opened the door, saw me, and came into my room. I said to myself, *This man isn't going to touch me while these people are here.* I was wrong! I had on a shirt and undergarments, and he came over to my bed. I turned in the opposite direction, hinting to him to leave me alone, but he kept moving toward me. At that moment, I became frozen and silent. He removed my undergarment and once again performed oral sex. He went a step further and tried to penetrate me, but I kept pulling away. I could faintly hear someone coming toward my room, and Junior immediately got up and went back to his room.

I couldn't understand how I could speak up and be disrespectful to Junior with others around. I had a voice, and I felt strengthened when others were around. However, when I was alone with him and no one else was around, I would be frozen in time and silent as a lamb.

One day I decided to walk to the corner store because I was crazy about Lemonheads candy. The store was about ten minutes' walking distance from the house. Junior pulled up beside me and told me to get in the car. I refused. He kept following me and told me he wanted to take me to a hotel. I kept walking and looking ahead. A car pulled up beside him and asked me if he was bothering me. I nodded my head yes, and the driver started to cuss him out while the woman in the passenger side asked me if I needed a ride home. I stated, "No!" That was the last incident I had with Junior.

Keeping Secrets and Moving On

It had been weeks since anyone had seen Junior, and no one asked about his whereabouts either. I never shared the horrible things that happened to me with Mrs. Henderson. She was unaware of what I endured with her husband. Fast-forward to a couple of days later, Mrs. Henderson came home with a new husband. The new man that Mrs. Henderson brought home was the opposite of Junior. They seemed to be more compatible, and he was older than her too.

As the fall of September 1985 approached, I started my eighth-grade school year at Bret Harte Middle School. I was nervous because Los Angeles is a fast-paced city. Mrs. Henderson took me clothing shopping to start the new school year. She loved me like her daughter. She'd take me to get my hair pressed and curled once a week, and I'd overhear her telling her peers about how she wanted me to remain with her forever. During this part of my life, my mother and I were reconnecting with each other. I visited my mother on weekends, and when I did, I never mentioned to her the dreadful things that happened at Mrs. Henderson's house. I was just glad to be reconnecting with my mother and have a great relationship with Mrs. Henderson.

Back to the situation at hand: the new school year. I imagined in my mind how the children would respond to me. I would be shy and didn't want to speak to anyone, and the other children would probably be mean to me. The other kids may have even known more about fashion and music trends, while I knew nothing about the fashion trends. Maybe I'd get along with some of my peers because I did know about the music trends, and most importantly, at this time I excelled in my academic abilities. I was so afraid that the children would make fun of me during this new school year because of my accent. And, of course, history would repeat itself.

Here's a Making My Spirit Smile Moment:

Mrs. Henderson had an old-school southern soul. She was very old fashioned and wasn't up to the current trends. Mrs. Henderson took care of me and made sure I had regular health checks—also making sure I had birth control. She was the representation of a good mom. One day Mrs. Henderson took me to see her friend, who was a licensed hairdresser. My hair was long, thick, nappy, and hard to manage. This woman bone straightened my hair, which reminded me of when I was a little girl and my grandmother would do the same on Saturday evenings for Sunday morning church services. After this lady had finished pressing my hair, you thought I had a relaxer in my hair. As a little girl, getting my hair done would uplift my spirit. It built my confidence, even if it was just for that moment.

Finding A Piece of Serenity

John 14:27, KJV

Peace I leave with you, my peace I give unto you: not as the world giveth, give I unto you. Let not your heart be troubled, neither let it be afraid.

By the early summer in June of 1986, I completed the eighth grade successfully. By midsummer, I reunited with my mother for good. I had mixed emotions because I had formed a bond with Mrs. Henderson. I came back home with my mom, and by this time my brother Bennie was in California too. My brother and I have a bond, but I didn't let him in on the abuse I had endured. The abuse was so common during that time that no one would discuss it. It seems like it was the norm to slap, punch, or cuss out children publicly. I believe today, those who grew up in my era and were abused have some form of mental illness. We need a way of developing healthy relationships and taking into account mental wellness.

During the summer I spent the majority of the time by the swimming pool. I would sit and watch my peers swim because I had no skills in swimming. Therefore, each day when the pool had fewer people in it, I would get in and try to swim. I watched others and tried to mimic their skills. One day one of my neighbors, Lamar, approached me about swimming. He was a young boy who lived in my complex. His family was amicable, and we became friends. Lamar had a stuttering problem, but that never kept me from being his friend. Lamar showed me around and introduced me to some other peers in the complex. They called me mermaid because I spent most of my time in the pool during my free time.

I was fascinated with water. I didn't know how to swim, but the water became soothing and refreshing to me. It calmed my mind and my thoughts. My desire is to one day have a home by a body of water.

As the end of summer was approaching, I still wasn't looking forward to the next school year. I would be attending Patrick Henry Middle School in Granada Hills,

MAKING MY SPIRIT SMILE

California, for my ninth-grade year. During that time, ninth grade was considered middle school; however, the academics credit went toward high school. This school was different from Bret Harte. The campus was well groomed, and their academic standards were elevated. This was the era of K-Swiss tennis shoes and the music of LL Cool J.

Do I Belong?
As I struggled to find a sense of belonging, I still maintained my grades. My history teacher was very inspiring to me. It seemed when I was depressed, he gave me encouraging words, maybe because I would do my assignments and was very respectful. The majority of the students weren't so fond of him because of the projects he would give us. His assignments required research and hours of study time.

The year flew by, and the ninth-grade promotion ceremony was approaching. It was June of 1987 when I finished my ninth-grade year with honors, and my mother was so proud of me. I remember her taking me shopping and buying me a dress with shoes, and on the day of graduation, I was happy because I had my mother and brother Bennie in the audience, cheering me on while my name was called as I walked across the stage. Although graduation day was exciting, the night before we graduated was Grand Night! Grand Night was when Great America shut down to the public and was only available to us ninth graders who'd be graduating. We'd be at the park all night having fun with our friends.

The summer was finally here, and I obtained my first babysitting job. In between me spending time with my friends, I would be by the swimming pool all the time. It reminded me of the previous summer, when one of Mrs. Henderson's sons would take us girls to the beach. The first time he took me to the beach, I was so excited. There was such peace while being by the oceanfront. That was the first time setting my eyes upon God's creation of the Pacific Ocean.

At the age of fifteen, I was timid but willing to reciprocate kindness. One day by the pool, I met this boy named Danny Lopez. I remember thinking he was black because of his skin tone. That wasn't the case. He was a dark-skinned Puerto Rican. During that summer, my friends and I spent time by the pool. Danny would join us in between visiting his mother. We began to spend a lot of time together, and there were very negative vibes coming from the other girls around.

In the middle of the summer, Danny and I sat by the pool and conversed with his mother. From out of the blue, in a joking manner, his mother stated, "I hope you both not having sex because I don't want half n****r grandbabies running around here." She laughed as if it was a joke, but undercover tried to figure out if Danny and I were sexually active. Now I must admit sometimes I would get angry inside, but I stayed respectful. Here's a woman with skin darker than mine who dared to say that to me. I reassured her that Danny and I weren't having sex. She explained that she had Danny at the age of fifteen, which at the moment, I calmed down and understood her reasoning for her question. Later that night, I addressed Danny about his mother's comments, and as for him, I gave him some "un-choice" words about his mother and him. As for Danny being her son, he defended her. I haven't spoken to her since that incident, and Danny and I stopped dating.

Here's a Making My Spirit Smile Moment:

My mother worked during the day as a nurse at Magnolia Gardens Nursing Home. There would be a time when my mother would have to work overtime. So she would pick me up, and those days would be the most memorable and happiest moments, being with her at her job. I was delighted to be around the elderly, which is why my heart goes out to the elderly. For some reason, I seemed to be attached to them. I didn't realize I was so drawn to the elderly until I got older. I sought in them what I wanted in my grandmother. One of my mother's coworkers was named Martinez. He was very flamboyant, loving, kind, full of joy, and most importantly, he would always make my spirit smile. He was very close to my mother and he treated me like he had known me all his life. At the time, I wasn't familiar with the homosexual lifestyle. I wasn't even aware that he was gay. Years later, Martinez died of complications of AIDS. I never judged his lifestyle because he was human and he treated me kindly. It is vital not to miss the opportunity for someone to bestow love. It is the heart of man, not the outer appearance, that can bring you pure, genuine happiness. For that reason, he made my spirit smile.

Acceptance and the Special In Me

John 1:11, KJV

He came unto his own, and his own received him not.

The fall of 1987 was the start of the tenth grade for me at Sylmar High School in Sylmar, California. My confidence was still about the same. I had very low self-esteem and I was very insecure and shy. As I entered the campus, I saw familiar faces from Olive Vista. I remember the first day standing in the line to get the printout of my classes. In my science class, there was a boy named Kevin who made my school year miserable. He was a big bully. He made fun of my accent and the way I looked. I didn't wear the latest fashion trends, but I was clean and had decent clothes. As this bullying continued, I would stay inside the study hall for recess and lunches. Although I enjoyed learning, I never had an outlet to speak about how cruel some of my peers were.

I would always pretend to be a Dallas Cowboys cheerleader. So when I learned the school was having cheerleading tryouts, it would be my time to shine. There were prerequisites to being a part of the squad: You must have a 3.0 GPA and good academic standing. I met all of the requirements. I devoted my time after school for three weeks to learn the routine. I didn't look like the other girls, I was the only black girl who had curves, but I knew the drill and felt I would have a squad position. It was my turn to go before the panel and audition. While I was on the platform, one of the judges started laughing at me. I could see one of the other judges. She was the captain on the team, and she nudged her peer to stop laughing. At that moment, my brief confidence was broken. As I finished, I walked out and couldn't wait to leave. I cried.

At that moment I knew I wasn't going to be selected and I knew I didn't fit the physical image criteria they wanted. A couple of months passed, and I had another opportunity to try out for another team: the drill team, and I made it on that squad. The boost of my confidence was what I needed to make a spot on the drill team. I felt so happy that I was finally doing something I looked forward to at school. During our football season, my brother Bennie, Paul, and Arc would be at the football game. For some reason, every time I saw Arc, I would smile, and he would smile back. I guess he sensed I had a crush on him, but he was too old for me. This man was a huge drug dealer, and the women flocked to him like bees to honey. During this time, some men didn't care if the girl was underage, but he did.

My Friends Arc and Juwana
My brother Bennie had his set of friends. One of his friends was named Arc. Bennie was the best friend of Arc's brother, Paul. Arc was about four years older than me. All the girls would light up when Arc was around. Now during this time, Bennie was getting into mischief being with Arc. I didn't know much about Arc, but I was aware that he wasn't anybody to underestimate. I recall a conversation I had with Arc. It was just he and I, and I told him that I liked him. He replied he knew this. He then said to me that I was charming and kind. I asked him if he would wait three years for me to become of age, and he told me he would.

Even though I knew he had other women, there was something special about him. Any other man I knew during that time wouldn't even consider my age. They would take advantage of me. And the odd thing is the other men weren't drug dealers; they'd be portrayed as upright citizens. After that, every time I would see Arc, he would stop and give me the most prominent, warmest smile and a hug. Not one time did he ever try to have a sexual encounter with me. I didn't agree with his lifestyle, nor did I agree with the involvement my brother began to be caught up in it—that particular kind of lifestyle comes with a price. And the following year, Arc was killed. My heart was broken because I truly loved him.

    Juwana was a popular girl at my school who was different from the rest. She was very kind, loving, uplifting, and always cheerful. Juwana was full of fashion and she also had thick, long, coarse hair. Juwana offered to do my hair at her home, which gave me a boost of confidence. She would even stand up against those who would bully me and tell them to stop. Today, Juwana still has a passion for hair. She is a successful mother, wife, and beauty shop business owner in California.

    During that summer of my eleventh-grade year of high school, I met many teenage guys who mistreated me and used me. I met this man I knew from the community. He was a womanizer, and I thought I could change him because I was a nice person. I was seventeen years old, and I found myself in a difficult situation. As I awoke one morning, I was feeling nausea. I thought nothing of it because I thought it was something I ate. I went about my daily activities. I went to school as usual, and a few months later, I realized I was pregnant. I didn't inform anybody that I was pregnant just yet.

Our homecoming game and dance were every year during the month of October. I attended every year, but this year I wasn't excited about going. I didn't want to be there because I was so depressed and no one had known about the pregnancy. My mother was so excited, so we went out to the stores, she purchased me a pretty dress, and she made an appointment at the beauty shop to get my hair done. Juwana was so happy to see me too. She came up to me and told me how beautiful I looked. She was smiling from ear to ear. I spent a couple of hours at the dance and then I went home.

Here's a Making My Spirit Smile Moment:

During the study hall, I met a boy named Tony Clark. Tony felt like an outsider too. He would discuss with me how he felt about his self-image. The students would tease him about his appearance, and he didn't feel confident about himself. We both were academic achievers, despite what challenges we both faced. He was one of my best friends. We hung out during school and on the weekend. Today, Tony is successful with a beautiful wife and children. My last conversation included him and his wife, and we were reminiscing on our school days.

Unconditional Love

Romans 5:8, NIV

But God demonstrates his own love for us in this: While we were still sinners, Christ died for us.

You hear people say they have "ride or die" friends or family members. Well in my case, my brother Bennie was just that. So in January of 1989, I told my brother, Bennie, I was pregnant. He informed my mother, and my mother asked me if it was true. I told her yes. My mother looked me in the eyes and told me I had two options: abortion; or get out of her house. In disbelief, I found myself walking alone down the streets of California. I didn't know what to do, so I decided to call my health education teacher.

Ms. Eleanor Bralver was my lifesaver. She was so loving toward all her students, and I felt her unconditional love for me as well. Ms. Bralver had finally answered her phone, and when she realized it was me, she could tell there was something wrong. Out of the blue, she asked me if I was pregnant. I told her yes. I also told her the response from my mother, which was so heartbreaking to me.

Although Ms. Bralver didn't drive during the nighttime, she came to pick me up. I spent the rest of the evening with her. The next morning, she arranged for me to move into a home for pregnant teenage girls. St. Anne's Maternity Home, located in Los Angeles, California, is a home for low-income and high-risk pregnant teens. They provided me with medical care, healthy, nutritious meals, snacks, parenting skills classes, and they made sure I gained an education.

Ms. Eleanor Bralver was the oldest full-time teacher that I knew and she retired at ninety-two. She died peacefully in her sleep on November 1, 2012, at the age of ninety-two. I know she had touched so many people, just as she touched my heart, and I thank her for making my spirit smile.

When not at the maternity home, I attended McAlister High School for pregnant teens Monday through

MAKING MY SPIRIT SMILE

Friday. You might ask where my baby's father was. He was killed after falling asleep behind the wheel coming home from work. Even though I was alone and depressed, I was able to continue my education without falling behind.

In school I used to sit in the back of the class so that the teacher wouldn't call on me. That was a bad idea. It seemed the more I hid, the more he would call upon me. During History class, I recall my teacher wanting everyone to read the book *The Color Purple*. I had never heard of this book before. After we read the book, he brought the movie to class, and we watched it. As a review of the film and the book, he would give us questions weekly. I assumed it was to see if we were paying attention and how much we'd retained. The scene I remember is when Nettie kissed her sister Celie when they were reunited. The teacher asked one of the students next to me how she felt about that. She was not very in touch with her emotions. She stated how ugly Celie was, and I saw that my teacher's expression was disturbed. He was trying to explain to her the greatness of their love. She kept saying, "She is too ugly to be kissed."

While I was sitting there, I said to myself, *I wish someone would love me in that type of way.*

The Birth of My Baby Girl

April 11, 1989 became the most significant and happiest moment of my life. It was the due date of my baby girl. However, on the night of March 21, 1989, I felt I needed to have a bowel movement. I thought nothing of this as I continued to feel this sensation throughout the night. The next morning, I would head to my appointment, but then I began to have very intense contractions. I informed the staff at the maternity home that I thought I was in labor. They timed my contractions, which were seven minutes apart. They agreed with my thoughts, and I then headed to my appointment.

I would go to a clinic affiliated with the Queen of Angels Hospital, and this would be the birthplace of my daughter. God had his hands upon me without me knowing it. When I arrived at the clinic, I immediately told my doctor, "I think I'm in labor." He did a physical check and confirmed I was in labor. I was transported to the hospital and admitted into my room. The doctor came in and broke my water sac. Afterward, the contractions became very intense. There are no words to describe the pain that I was feeling. I was alone with no one to comfort me. Fear was setting in because the medication they'd administered wasn't smoothening the pain. I dilated to five centimeters, and you have to dilate to ten centimeters to deliver a baby. Dilation is when your cervix expands and opens for the baby to pass through without complications. Because I suffered in pain for so many hours, that presented a risk of complications to my baby. So the doctor changed the plan of birth and they performed a cesarean procedure; this is when the woman gets an incision up above her bikini area and the doctors remove the baby.

The cesarean procedure took about fifteen to twenty minutes. When they pulled out my daughter, tears flowed uncontrollably down my face.

John 16:21, NIV
"A woman giving birth to a child has pain because her time has come; but when her baby is born she forgets the anguish because of her joy that a child is born into the world."

I can't recall anything after the moment my daughter was born. As I awoke, I looked to my left, and a nurse was sitting next to me. She was monitoring the mechanical ventilator that was connected to me. When my daughter was born, I stopped breathing. I don't remember being unconscious at all. I remained on the mechanical ventilator for twenty-four hours after the birth of my baby girl.

Love—nothing is more significant. I told myself that my daughter was going to know her mother loves her. She smelled like the air after a spring dew. I felt love without conditions, love that seals till death, love that can't be described. I knew it was my duty to provide, protect, and show her the love that wasn't given to me. I was determined that my daughter would hear "I love you" every day. I said it all the time, to the point that my daughter responds, "I know, Mom—and everyone knows!" I also had the mindset that if anyone harmed my daughter, we both would see each other's soul in hell. I was determined that no one would hurt my child. I became overly protective of my daughter, which can present a different kind of challenge.

I became so overly protective of my daughter. Because I had not sought help or counsel from my past, I found myself being possessive of my baby girl. I frequently called her on the phone. I had to meet everyone who crossed her path: her teachers, friends, everyone. I became paranoid. I had good intentions, but I was smothering her to the point where she wanted to escape, and later in life, when she got older—she did. She went to Stillman College in Alabama. Not only did my daughter graduate from high school a year early, but she also received her associate's degree at the age of seventeen, and when she did, we celebrated the entire week. She received so many scholarships from so many different schools. I am so very proud of my firstborn and all of my children's accomplishments.

> **Here's a Making My Spirit Smile Moment:**
>
> During my stay at St. Anne's Maternity Home, my brother Bennie would keep in touch with me. I was in my craving stages. During that time, I would crave a Big Mac from McDonald's. The Big Mac was two for five dollars, and they tasted better then than they do now. I would call my brother and tell him I would like a Big Mac from McDonald's. He would drive for about twenty-five minutes from San Fernando Valley to bring me two Big Macs. He wouldn't complain, which made me very happy—and thank you, brother, for making my tummy smile.

Abandonment. Isolation. Rejection. Abuse. No love.

Making My Spirit Smile

THE REVELATION

Tiffany Jackson

S.H.E. PUBLISHING, LLC

MAKING MY SPIRIT SMILE

Captivity

Jeremiah 1:5

says how God knew you from the beginning of time. He knew the moment you would be born and the moment you would die. He knows every hair on your head—every trial, hardship, waves of laughter, disappointments, and victories you will experience. He needs someone willing to go through the challenges that life may bring to help someone else out of captivity.

As I walked into the doors of hell with my heels and sexy stride, the only woman with curves, I made my way past the flashing lights and down the hall into the room where I became a new woman. And as I walked out onto the stage to position myself next to the pole in front of the occupied table and chairs, I'd encounter the major earthquake that shook me which led me to stripping.

"I'd like to introduce: Yummy Yummy!"

To be continued...

ACKNOWLEDGEMENTS

First, I give thanks to God's hedge of divine protection over my life and for planting the seed in me to gain the courage to share my story. I also thank all who, in one way or another, contributed to the completion of the Making My Spirit Smile project, which includes my Bishop, Damen Bennett, and Pastor Staci Bennet of the Fresh Oil Ministries located in East Chicago, Indiana.

I also give thanks to S.H.E. Publishing, LLC, and Elite Authors for assisting with guiding me through the process of making my dream become a reality. To Evita Howard, I thank her for connecting me to this professional publishing house.

And to my friends; Beverly Newsome, Jackie Calloway, Kikko Smith, Emmanuel Knight of the New Paradise Family, Apostle Rosita Simmons, Evangelist Jairous Simmons, Bishop Avery Austin of Total Deliverance Family, and the remaining family of Fresh Oil Ministries—my deepest gratitude for your real friendships.

To my caring, loving, and supportive family who encouraged me and prayed for me throughout this new

MAKING MY SPIRIT SMILE

journey. To name a few, I thank my daughter Brittany Jackson and her husband Marlowe Jackson (my son in love), my daughter India Alexis, my son Emmanuel Mbachu, my grandson Kamrin Hilsan, and my Goddaughter Shonda Bowerman. This book has also been greatly inspired by my mother, who I know is smiling upon me from the heavens. Although she is not physically with us, I feel her spirit, and it continues to make my spirit smile.

ABOUT THE AUTHOR

Born to Shirley Jean Johnson and Bennie Eddie Jackson, Tiffany Zabrina Jackson grew up in Hickory, Mississippi and the southern cities of California. She is a younger sister of two brothers, Bennie Jackson and John Johnson. She has three amazing children: Brittany Jackson (Marlowe), India Alexis, and Emmanuel Mbachu. They continue to be her inspiration and support system.

In Jackson's lifetime, she has earned her associate's degree in Child and Family Education and is currently working on

MAKING MY SPIRIT SMILE

her bachelor's degree in Human Services. She has been working in the medical field, where she takes care of patients with several elements. In the interim, she has become an author with the goal of continuing to see where this new journey will take her.

Jackson's hobbies consist of going to the beach, reading, traveling, listening to music, sitting on the couch watching old movies, being involved in and serving the community, and spending quality time with family. She is truly a woman with a big heart and a kind spirit.

TIFFANY JACKSON

MAKING MY SPIRIT SMILE

www.ingramcontent.com/pod-product-compliance
Lightning Source LLC
Chambersburg PA
CBHW061202070526
44579CB00009B/97